Taming Wild Thoughts

Wilfred Bion
Stockholm, 1963

Taming Wild Thoughts

Wilfred R. Bion

edited by
Francesca Bion

London
KARNAC BOOKS

First published in 1997 by
H. Karnac (Books) Ltd.
58 Gloucester Road
London SW7 4QY

British Library Cataloguing in Publication Data

Bion, Wilfred R. (Wilfred Ruprecht), 1887–1979
    Taming wild thoughts
    1. Psychoanalysis
    I. Title
    150.1'95

    ISBN 1-85575-168-2

Edited, designed, and produced by Communication Crafts

Printed in Great Britain by BPCC Wheatons Ltd, Exeter

10 9 8 7 6 5 4 3 2

CONTENTS

FOREWORD

Parthenope Bion Talamo

The two unpublished pieces by W. R. Bion contained in this booklet have several themes in common, although they were composed in different circumstances and at quite a length of time from each other. The first is a paper, 'The Grid', which was given to the British Psycho-Analytical Society on 2 October 1963, while the second is an untitled transcript by F. Bion of tape recordings made in 1977.

The principal theme is that of the classification (and hence the taming) of the psychoanalytic objects that belong to the domain of ideas, as Bion defines them at the end of the first chapter of *Elements of Psycho-Analysis* (1963), and the ways in which they can be used. The short paper would seem to have been written at much the same time as *Elements of Psycho-Analysis* and might constitute an early draft which later grew into the book. My reasons for thinking this are based on a fairly detailed comparison of the two texts. In the first place, the Grid itself has a slight change in it: in the paper printed here, Column 5 is indicated as Oedipus, whereas the Grid printed in *Elements of Psycho-Analysis* and onwards has this column labelled as Inquiry, as though the author had decided to opt for the more general category, of which 'Oedipus' is simply a special case, as the discussion of this column in the book shows. Secondly, if you try to read *Elements of Psycho-Analysis* 'innocently', so to speak, as though you did not know that the book contains the first and main detailed discussion of the Grid, you will discover that Chapters 5 and 6 discuss the horizontal and then the vertical axes of the Grid without mentioning the word 'grid' for a full nine pages, and when it is brought in towards the end of Chapter 6, the term itself is not discussed at all. It is almost as though an introductory piece had been left out at the beginning of Chapter 5. I do not think that the paper printed here constitutes the missing introduction—it is far too long and detailed for that—but I suspect that Bion may have had the paper in his mind, as something 'already written', while he was preparing *Elements of Psycho-Analysis* for the press and did not feel the need to enlarge further on the introductory aspects in the book itself.

It would not be the first time that something of this sort occurred in Bion's published writings: the passages in *Cogitations* (1994) on alpha-elements, dream-work-alpha, and beta-elements seem to come into a similar category, that of a full discussion of terms which was then left out of the text to be published—or taken out, perhaps, as being too introspective? In any case, I think it is fair to say that one's understanding of both the Grid and the abovementioned concepts is made easier by studying what could perhaps be thought of as being the 'parings', which Bion whittled away from his finished writings.

As it stands, this particular paper is a model of clarity and highlights some background characteristics of Bion's thought, which he was never to abandon. The most important of these shows through when he makes explicit the fact that what he says about the patient's development of thoughts or his usage of them can also apply to the analyst, who, inasmuch as he is a human being, also suffers from the vagaries and limitations of the human capacity for thinking and communication. I do not mean that Bion is talking about what is called countertransference, either in the strict sense of the term or the looser one that it generally has today, but that he was working on a system that would help him to track down after a session, in a moment of relative peace and quiet, what had happened during the session. And the things that happen during the session include just as much the analyst's thought processes and the use he makes of these as it does the patient's: and they both need scrutiny at the end of the session.

How things moved around, developed, evolved (or failed to do so) was a never-failing source of interest to Bion, and I do not think that it is too fanciful to see an early precursor of the Grid in the description that he gives, in *Experiences in Groups* (1961; in 'Intra-Group Tensions in Therapy', towards the end of the section on 'Discipline for the Neurotic'), of his visualization of '. . . the projected organization of the training wing as if it were a framework enclosed within transparent walls. Into this space the patient would be admitted at one point, and the activities within that space would be so organized that he could move freely in any direction according to the resultant of his conflicting impulses. . . . As a result, his behaviour could be trusted to give a fair indication of his effective will and aims . . .' (Bion, 1961, pp. 14–15). The Grid itself plots the evolution and use of ideas and not the development of men, but the 'visualization' behind both the fantasy and the Grid is not substantially different in its aims in both cases.

Another interesting link between *Experiences in Groups* and the present paper can be found in the discussion of the importance of the circumference of the circle as a factor in the fecundity of thought: a brief mention of this (Bion, 1961, p. 13) in the earlier book, later to be picked up again in a cursory and almost joking fashion in *Transformations* (1965, p. 111), receives a far more detailed treatment in this version of the Grid. There is another sense, too, in which *Transformations* seems to be foreshadowed by this paper. It contains the discussion of the 'transformation' of the field of poppies that becomes the starting point for the 1965 book; it also introduces the symbols for short-hand indication of the analyst's and patient's transformations.

Why Bion never published this paper, which has an important linking function between the work that preceded it and that which came later, as well as constituting a remarkably clear discussion of the whys and wherefores of the Grid itself, and then later, in 1971 (Bion, 1977), produced another one with the same title, remains a mystery. The 1971 paper grew out of a talk that he gave to the Los Angeles Psychoanalytic Society in April of that year and is unusual in that it contains some fairly detailed clinical material. It is also rather more discursive in style than the present paper (as are the two transcripts that follow the latter in this collection), and I think that on the whole, although there is a certain amount of overlap, the two Grid papers complement each other in a rather interesting fashion. They might even be said to make up the two viewpoints of a possible binocular vision (for the reader), 1963 and 1971, England and California, inception of the Grid and a re-visitation of it. (With *Nachträglichkeit*? Perhaps.)

The two transcripts, on the other hand, seem to have been intended as the first chapters of a book of which no more is known; the recordings were made on two consecutive days in late May 1977, when *A Memoir of the Future* (1991) was already finished and Bion was working on his autobiography, but they are different in kind from both of these. In the first 'chapter', he takes up the idea of stray and wild thoughts and how to capture them and intro-duces the concept of beta-element, in an almost whimsical fashion, as a 'box' into which to put one sort of captured stray. The dis-cussion that develops links up with the Grid, as it deepens and develops the notions of alpha- and beta-elements, dream thought, and rhythmic, non-verbal communication. Bion goes on to show something of what he had in mind when he talks of language achievement, as a sort of high-point of sophisticated and efficacious communication, and then returns to the physical level, beta-elements, ending with a discussion of archaic vestigial aspects of the mind. The style is very discursive—conversational, almost—and might be thought of as rambling, but it is in itself a good example of the validity of the 'large circumference' of a circular argument, since the return to the theme of beta-elements towards the end of the chapter is notably enriched by all that has occurred 'on the way'. (I have often thought that Bion's concept of a circular argument was well illustrated by the circular form of Joyce's *Finnegan's Wake*.)

The second 'chapter' takes up the problem of evaluation; start-ing again from sensorial data, beta-elements, which Bion seems to assume in a relaxed sort of way as a non-questionable 'given' on which to build his architectonics of thought, he moves on to the question of psycho-analytic supervision. Several points come up for discussion on the first section, which might be headed 'specula-tive imagination'—another term for wild thoughts: the relevance of the past only inasmuch as it obtrudes on the present; the deep and profound respect for the patient's present, for his presence in the room, and for the experience of this, which the analyst can have if he allows himself to do so; the noxiousness of hopes and fears, tying up with memory and desire but from a slightly different angle; the minimum conditions necessary for analytic work to be done.

The second section takes up the theme of speculative reason— that is, the discipline that has to be applied to the speculative imagination—and is followed by a brief sortie into what Bion calls reconstruction, but which turns rather rapidly into a short essay on theory leading on to a discussion of unconscious thought that has never been conscious, dubbed the 'inaccessible state of mind'.

Despite the recurrent themes in the two pieces presented here, their style is completely different, and the transcript probably reflects Bion's greater confidence in the validity of psychoanalysis as he practised it, and consequently his own greater self-confidence. One might say again that the transcripts represent the ending point, coincident with the beginning (represented by 'The Grid') of another circle with an ever wider circumference, from the early formulations of alpha- and beta-elements to the later ones, with all his maturing analytical experiences on the way round.

Turin
April 1997

THE GRID

Introduction

In 1994 Dr Rosa Beatriz, from Rio de Janeiro, sent me a copy of this paper, which had been given to her by Dr Hans Thorner in 1971, when she was in London. I am grateful to her for resurrecting this piece, especially as it had disappeared from my records—and my memory—and has not been previously published, with the exception of its inclusion in a magazine containing the contributions to a workshop held in Rio de Janeiro in November 1994. Bion presented it at a scientific meeting of the British Psycho-Analytical Society on 2 October 1963; I believe that a hand-written date on the first page, 2/10/63, was added by Dr Thorner.

It was written after the publication of *Learning from Experience* (1962b), in which the Grid is not mentioned, although Bion had been working on the idea for some time before that. We discussed various possible names for the new 'offspring' about which he was then expressing all the usual enthusiasm aroused by a new invention—followed ultimately by the equally usual realization of its defects (see Bion, *Two Papers*, 1977, p. 16).

In this 1963 paper, his aim is to give a clear and detailed explanation of the Grid's construction and its uses; this he does admirably and does not 'digress', as he could be said to do in the 1971 version, which is twice as long. That paper contains some vivid clinical material and a fairly lengthy discussion of six myths (Row C constructs); he laid increasing stress on the importance of their use from 1963 (*Elements of Psycho-Analysis*, 1963) onwards.

He produced plenty of evidence to highlight the deficiencies of the Grid: 'I can say that an early casualty in trying to use the Grid is the Grid itself.' But he goes on, 'Nevertheless, its use has made it easier for me to preserve a critical and yet informative, illuminating attitude to my work' (Bion, 1977, p. 6). In 1974, in Rio de Janeiro, he said, 'The Grid is a feeble attempt to produce an instrument. . . . I think it is good enough to know how bad it is, how unsuitable for the task for which I have made it' (Bion, 1974/75). And as late as 1977, in New York, he stated: 'As soon as I had got the Grid out of my system I could see how inadequate it is . . . the satisfaction does not last for long.' Asked if it was difficult, he replied, 'Not for me—only a waste of time because it doesn't really correspond with the facts I am likely to meet' (Bion, 1980). Although it was certainly not his intention, these remarks were discouraging, to say the least; on the other hand, in San Paulo in 1973, he reacted with obvious interest and enthusiasm to a question about a possible amplification of the Grid (see Bion, *Brazilian Lectures*, 1974/75, pp. 41–42). In reply he spoke of visualizing the Grid as repeating itself as a helix. Again in San Paulo in 1978, he touched on an interesting extension of the Grid (see *Bion in New York and Sao Paulo*, 1980, pp. 91, 92): he imagined it turned so that 'the distances between the lines would become very fine' and called it a Grating.

Bion emphasized that the Grid is not a theory, nor should it be used during the session, but it can be used to advantage 'in relative isolation from attack'. He gave a warning: '. . . it cannot do harm, provided it is not allowed to intrude in the analyst–analysand relationship as a theory about the patient which is stored up and then discharged like a missile in battle.'

It may be helpful to set out the uses to which, he believed, and indeed found through his own experience, the Grid could be put. They are these:

1. to keep the analyst's intuition in training;
2. to help in impressing the work of the sessions on the memory;
3. to increase the accuracy of observations;
4. to make it easier to bridge the gap between events of an analysis and their interpretation;
5. as a 'game' for psycho-analysts to set themselves exercises as a method of developing their capacity for intuition;
6. to help in developing a method of written recording analogous to mathematical communication, even in the absence of the object;
7. as a prelude to psycho-analysis, not as a substitute for it;
8. to provide a mental climbing-frame on which psycho-analysts could exercise their mental muscles;
9. as an instrument for classifying and ultimately understanding statements.

F.B.

1963

T his paper is to introduce a method I have found useful in thinking about problems that arise in the course of psycho-analytical practice.

We are familiar with anxieties arising in the course of treating patients and of the need to deal with these anxieties by being ourselves analysed. Today I am concerned with an aspect of this that seems to have received little or no attention, namely, what might be called reasonable anxiety that arises when it is clearly important to solve a problem that is by virtue of its complexity very difficult to solve. Because of our work, there is a tendency to regard such anxiety as counter-transference and to forget that it may also be proper to the search for an adequate response to a danger. My approach must not be regarded as implying that there is any less need for the analyst's personal analysis. What I shall say should in fact contribute to the approach through personal analysis.

My subject does not belong directly to the sphere of work done in analytic situations or throw much light on how to record sessions. Yet it has a bearing on the work of the session because the procedures I am about to advocate do help to keep the analyst's intuition in training, so to speak, and do help in impressing the work of the sessions on the memory. Later perhaps it might help in developing a method of written recording analogous to that enjoyed by the mathematician who can record his findings and use the record for communication and further work on his findings even in the absence of the object.

The instrument that I have elaborated for this task is the Grid (Figure 1).

It will be seen that there are two axes, one vertical marked A–H, the other horizontal, which is numbered 1, 2, 3, . . . to n. The vertical axis is genetic and is divided roughly into phases of sophistication.

	1 Defini-tory Hypo-thesis	2 ψ	3 Nota-tion	4 Atten-tion	5 Oedip.*	6 Action	. . . n . . .
A β-Elements	A1	A2				A6	An
B α-Elements	B1	B2	B3	B4	B5	B6	Bn
C Dream Thoughts Myth, Dream, Model	C1	C2	C3	C4	C5	C6	Cn
D Pre-conception	D1	D2	D3	D4	D5	D6	Dn
E Conception	E1	E2	E3	E4	E5	E6	En
F Concept	F1	F2	F3	F4	F5	F6	Fn
G Scientific Deductive System	G1	G2	G3	G4			
H Algebraic Calculus		H2					

*Later changed to 'Inquiry'. See 'The Grid', in Bion, *Two Papers* (1977).

FIGURE 1: The Grid

The meaning is broadly indicated by the terms I have used. They are borrowed from philosophy and elsewhere but must not be taken to have the meaning with which they are already invested in their rigorous employment in the discipline from which they are borrowed; they must be regarded as intended ultimately to have a meaning appropriate to psycho-analysis.

The horizontal axis relates to 'uses' to which the elements in the genetic axis are put. I have annotated the numbers in an imprecise manner similar to that with which I have used terms to annotate the vertical axis. When an element in the vertical axis appears to be identical with that in the horizontal axis the confusion will disappear if it is remembered that the term in the vertical axis is intended to denote a phase in development, whereas in the horizontal axis it is intended to denote the use that is made of the element.

The Grid is intended to aid the analyst in the categorization of statements. It is not a theory, though psycho-analytical theories have been used to construct it, but has the status of an instrument. A word or two is necessary to explain my use of the term 'statement'.

By 'statement' I mean anything from an inarticulate grunt to quite elaborate constructions such as this paper itself. A single word is a statement, a gesture or grimace is a statement; in short it is any event that is part of communication between analyst and analysand, or any personality and itself.

The horizontal axis is incomplete and is accordingly divided into columns marked to indicate that the series is extensible. Whether it should be so extended, and if so in what manner, is left to be determined in the course of its use. The existing columns have been used by me and I do not think they should be lightly discarded. They were devised primarily with what I have called a K link in mind, but their usefulness is unimpaired for L and H. I may explain that K is intended to denote the domain of learning from experience, L to denote the domain of love in all its aspects, and H the domain of hate. The domains are assumed to overlap, despite the rigidity that the signs may seem to impart. The letters L, H, and K are to facilitate discussion in a manner similar to that described later when I discuss α and β.

The horizontal axis is intended to relate to a statement that is constant; its meaning changes only because its use has changed in accordance with the column in which it is felt to be appropriate to place it.

Column 1 is subtitled 'definitory hypothesis'. This term, like many others I use, is not to be taken as possessing the meaning it already has alone and unmodified. It is used to indicate an aspect of statements that belong to, or are placed in, that category. Statements to which this category is appropriate mark that elements previously regarded as unrelated are believed to be constantly conjoined (Hume, *Hume's Enquiries*; Poincaré, *Science and Method*) and to have coherence. A statement in this column should be considered to have significance but not meaning. The term *'cat'* in this context indicates that the observer has become convinced of the constant conjunction of, say, fur, life, eyes, and so on. This constant conjunction is felt *not* to be some previous constant conjunction (Aristotle, Topics, VI, 4, 141, & 26 sqq.), and the statement is intended to bind the elements constantly conjoined and to define the area within which the conjoined elements reside; it is in this respect that it resembles what is ordinarily considered to be a definitory hypothesis. From the fact that the definitory statement does not refer to an earlier conjunction springs the objection, sometimes made, that a definition is negative. The binding of a constant conjunction and the implication of significance it carries with it makes possible the next step in learning, the task of finding out what 'cat' means.

Column 2 is to categorize the 'use' to which a statement—of whatever kind it may be and however untrue in the context—is put with the intention of preventing a statement, however true in the context, that would involve modification in the personality and its outlook. I have arbitrarily used the sign ψ to emphasize the close relationship of this 'use' to phenomena known to analysts as expressions of 'resistance'.

Column 3 contains the categories of statements that are used to record a fact. Such statements are fulfilling the function described by Freud as notation and memory (Freud, 1911b).

Column 4 represents the 'use' described by Freud, in the same paper, as the function of attention. The statement *'cat'* would then be used to ensure sensitiveness to a repetition of the constant conjunction. Statements properly regarded as appropriate to Column 4 relate to constant conjunctions that *have* been previously experienced, and the 'use' represented by Column 4 categories differs in this respect from the 'use' represented by Column 1.

Column 5, particularly the gloss 'Oedipus', requires some explanation. In so far as it represents a 'use' similar to Column 4, it may be regarded as redundant. I am loth to discard it, partly because it serves as an example of a 'use' that makes me unwilling to formulate 'uses' prematurely. A criticism of Oedipus implicit in the story (I refer specifically to the Sophoclean version) is the obstinacy with which he pursues his inquiry. This aspect of curiosity may seem unimportant to the philosopher of science, but it is of significance clinically and therefore worth including with Columns 3 and 4 as representing something that is more than a difference of intensity, just as 4 (Attention) is more than an intense 3 (Notation). A situation that will serve as an example is an occasion when the analyst has to distinguish between allowing himself too easily to abandon an approach to the solution of a problem and pressing it beyond the patients' capacity for endurance.

The last column, which I have annotated 'Action', also requires comment. It refers to those phenomena that resemble motor discharge intended to unburden 'the mental apparatus of accretions of stimuli' (Freud, 1911b, p. 221). To qualify for inclusion in this category, the action should be an expression of a theory that is readily detectable—otherwise it cannot be described as a 'use' of a theory. The problem of clarifying Grid categories arises from the fact that clarification must depend on experience. Inclusion in a Grid category is itself a statement by the analyst: all Grid categories may be regarded as having the quality of Column 1 categories in that they are significant but cannot be held to have meaning until experience invests them with it.

The first two rows of the genetic axis may be discussed together: β-elements and α-elements are intended to denote objects that are unknown and therefore may not even exist. By speaking of α-elements, β-elements, and α-function, I intend to make it possible to discuss something, or to talk about it, or think about it before knowing what it is. At the risk of suggesting a meaning, when I wish the sign to represent something of which the meaning is to be an open question, to be answered by the analyst from his own experience, I must explain that the term 'β-element' is to cover phenomena that may not reasonably be regarded as thoughts at all. Included in this category are the phenomena that I have previously tried to describe in a discussion of bizarre objects (see *Learning from Experience*). The problem, from my point of view, arises because of the tendency for meaning to creep in prematurely. Ideally, any meaning that the term accumulates should derive from analytic practice and from analytic practice alone. Much the same is true of the α-element, except that this term should cover phenomena that are reasonably considered to be thoughts. I would regard them as elements that make it possible for the individual to have what Freud described as dream thoughts.

Row C includes dreams and other possible organized systems of dream thoughts. Myth is to be included, together with organized structures that are primitive forms of model.

All rows except the first are to represent categories of statements that are unsaturated—that is, capable of accumulating meaning. In this respect it may seem misleading to describe Row E as consisting of pre-conceptions to the exclusion of the remaining rows, for they are capable also of functioning as pre-conceptions (because pre-conception may refer either to a phase of development or a 'use') in an ascending order of sophistication. As I have said elsewhere, I do not think it likely that in analytic practice an analyst would discover anything that would pass muster, by any rigorous standard of accepted scientific method, for inclusion in Rows G and H. Nevertheless I think it important that these categories should exist, although it involves the paradox of employing or appearing to employ rigorous standards loosely. One reason for such categories lies in the fact that statements that, under analytic scrutiny, turn out to be loose statements are often employed by scientists and philosophers as if they were rigorous.

If a competent artist, using the artistic conventions familiar to Western civilization, were to paint a field of poppies, we should have no difficulty in saying it was a field of poppies. Why should this be so? The lines on a straight stretch of railway would be thought of as being parallel, yet we should recognize a painting in which they were represented by lines that converged. And so on.

I propose to use the term 'transformation' to describe the process, whatever it is, by which the painter has transformed his experience into oil and pigment disposed on the canvas. But I don't wish the term to mean what it would mean if I said a building had been transformed by a painter and decorator—that the field of poppies has been used as raw material for the manufacture of canvas, oil, and pigment. Nor do I mean to suggest that the observer of the painting thinks he has discovered the source of the raw material if he describes the painting as a field of poppies. In short, I propose to use the term 'transformation', in accordance with my description of elements in Column 1, as a binding together of a constant conjunction so that I can proceed, with the help of this term, to find out what the constant conjunction means. The constant conjunction to which my term relates occurs in psycho-analytic sessions, and I hope to bind it by this term and to communicate the experience to the reader. If I can succeed in my aim, I hope that those to whom I communicate it will be able to discover the meaning of the term 'transformation' and the emotional experience whose constantly conjoined elements I have represented by the term.

As a first step towards understanding the meaning, I shall resume my discussion of my model, the field of poppies and the painting that represents it, and my 'myth' that an artist has effected a transformation. The realization—i.e. the field of poppies and all similar objects—I shall represent by the sign 'O'.

In analysis I shall assume that the medium for the transformation is conversational English. By this I mean that grammatical and verbal exactitude is not to be looked for, and that mien and gestures—muscular movements—are included in the expression 'conversational English'. I shall further assume that communication is being made by patient and analyst. Finally, I shall assume that the analytically relevant part of the communications of both patient and analyst is about an emotional experience. For brevity, I shall use the following signs:

$T\alpha p$ signifies the process of transformation in the mind of the patient; $T\alpha a$ the same process in the mind of the analyst. Similarly, $T\beta p$ and $T\beta a$ represent the finished product, the result of the process of transformation, the analytic counterpart of the artist's painting. In our work, O must always be an emotional experience, for the assumption in psycho-analysis is that patients come for help with, and therefore presumably want to talk about, an emotional difficulty.

There are a number of interesting ramifications into which I cannot enter here. It is only necessary to consider questions such as those touching the nature of the artist's communication—whether he is attempting to record a particular landscape or his emotions about it, whether he does or does not wish to influence the public to whom the finished product is to be displayed, and so forth—to see the complexities that are involved. I shall therefore introduce one more point only, namely the question with which I started: why is there no difficulty in recognizing that a painting represents a field of poppies? I shall answer it by saying that there is always something in the transformation that is invariant both to O and Tβ, the finished product.

To return now to the Grid: I have said that it is an instrument for classifying and ultimately understanding statements. The object of my discussion of transformations is to introduce the idea that in analytic practice all statements must be regarded as transformations. Even a single word such as 'cat', with its accompanying movements, intonation, and so forth, is a transformation of an emotional experience, O, into the final product, Tβp. It is for the analyst to decide when the transformation is complete. He may think that this point has been reached with the utterance of a single word or after a verbal communication lasting for a considerable period.

The analyst's communications may be scrutinized by the same mode of analysis as that to which I have subjected the communications of the patient. But it must be borne in mind that his aim is to give an interpretation. Any interpretation is a statement and a transformation but it is also something more and less than both, and the term 'interpretation' should apply only to something peculiar to the practice of the psycho-analyst. I hope that use of the Grid to classify the analyst's statement, and scrutiny of the transformation, may lead to a clearer understanding of the qualities that are necessary before a statement can be properly regarded as a psycho-analytical interpretation.

I have attempted so far to formulate some of the elements involved in observation. They may all be included under the heading of determining three things: the significant, its meaning, and the interpretation of the meaning. It will be seen therefore that I wish to establish a distinction between meaning and psycho-analytic interpretation. To put it in another way, I think it helpful to make a distinction between what the patient's meaning in conversation would be, and what the interpretation of that is when it is a psycho-analysis and not an ordinary conversation.

To summarize: the analyst is concerned with making observations on behaviour in which a number of components may be distinguished. These are: the genesis and use of the statements, the nature of the statement as a transformation, the process by which the transformation is effected (Tαp), the end-product of the transformation (Tβp), invariants, and the Grid category of the transformation.

The analyst, to observe correctly, must be sensitive to as many of the phenomena that are included in these headings as possible. The more nearly he is able to approximate to this ideal, the nearer he is to the first essential in psycho-analysis—or, for that matter, any other science—namely, correct observation. The complement of the first essential is the last essential—correct interpretation. By 'first' essential I mean not only priority in time but priority in importance, because if an analyst can observe correctly there is always hope; it is of course a big 'if'. Without the last essential he is not an analyst, but if he has the first essential he may become one in time; without it he can never become one, and no amount of theoretical knowledge will save him. This brings me to reconsideration of the nature of interpretation.

Interpretation is a special case: it is like all other statements in analysis in that it can have any of the characteristics, though ideally it should not, that I have attributed to the statement, and, like all statements, it is a transformation. It is unlike in that it should have K characteristics and be classifiable in a restricted range of rows. It should, on the face of it, be restricted to Columns 3, 4, and, more rarely, 1 and 5. When I deal later with the psycho-analytical game (see p. 20), I shall show that it may be placed hypothetically in any Grid category that the reviewing analyst thinks might stimulate a useful train of thought. With these points I shall deal after discussing some of the implications of my proposal to regard only particular aspects of events in an analytical session as peculiarly the province of psycho-analytical observations. This is already implicit in the application of psycho-analytical theories: I wish to make it explicit as a theory of observations that are to be matched with psycho-analytical theories. For, if observation is sound, the conclusion that certain observed phenomena appear to approximate to a psycho-analytical theory will also be sound. But the soundness of the conclusion is impaired if the theory, which is always a pre-conception (Row D), colours the selection of the facts to be observed. The object of the Grid is to aid in developing a pre-conception, in the analyst, that is *not* directly psycho-analytical so that the observations made are not such that they are bound to approximate to a psycho-analytical theory. For if the pre-conception is psycho-analytical, there is clearly a risk that the observations made under such a pre-conception appear to approximate to a psycho-analytical theory because they in fact derive from it. Such a condition amounts to circular argument. I have no objection to the circular argument and shall discuss the nature of its dangers later (see p. 18). For the present I shall assume the desirability of avoiding a circular argument to return to the consideration of 'statements'. Those, as I have said, must be considered to be 'transformations' in the sense in which I have used the term above, but, in addition to the characteristics already described, they must also be recognized as having the character of a theory. In other words, the objects of psycho-analytic study (psycho-analytic objects) have the characteristics I have bound by the term 'statement', the characteristics I have bound by the term 'transformation', and now also the characteristics I wish to 'bind' by the term 'theory'. So I shall now discuss the term 'theory'.

Reference to the Grid will show that I might equally well choose the term 'pre-conception' (Row D) but prefer a term that would be appropriately categorized in a relatively more sophisticated category.

The theory, no matter what the statement (or formulation) may be or what characteristics it has derived from its nature as a transformation, is never right or wrong: it *is* meaningful. Much confusion exists amongst scientists through beliefs that theories are right or wrong and accordingly require to be validated by empirical testing. I must therefore make it clear that this approach is unrewarding and that any supposition on which it is based must be replaced, as far as psycho-analysis is concerned and in the context of this discussion, by the supposition that the psycho-analytical object (= statement–transformation–theory) must be regarded in its theoretical aspects as if it were a formulation binding a constant conjunction. To make my point clear, I shall choose an extreme example.

A patient, though aware of the approach of a car, walked out in front of it, was knocked down, and sustained minor injuries. This result was apparently quite unexpected. Many of his statements had prepared me to expect that he was dominated at the time of the event by the conviction that he was a puff of flatus.

The statements amounting to an assertion that he was a puff of flatus constitute an example of what I mean by theory.

From the point of view of the patient, this was not a theory that needed validation to test the truth or otherwise of the statement. (I shall assume from now on that the reader is aware of the special sense in which I use the term 'statement'). According to my theory of the statement, he was engaged in establishing its meaning. Furthermore, the 'statement' was not only the verbal account he attempted to give me but was, in my opinion—although I was not there to see—probably also the correct term to apply to the event itself: it was a statement indistinguishable from the many statements to which, as his analyst, I am a witness. I shall now consider the implications of regarding this as a statement.

Let us first take the point that the statement is never right or wrong but only meaningful. Any view that the episode was an empirical testing of a hypothesis leads to a dead end. But if it is regarded as a statement designed first to bind a constant conjunction and thereby to take the first step in establishing the meaning of the constant conjunction, certain aspects of the episode become clearer. The accident and its attendant conclusions do not contribute meaning to the statement that he is a puff of flatus. For such a contribution to be possible, a realization must be found that approximates to the statement. In this respect the situation is in no way different from that presented by a highly sophisticated statement such as the mathematical formula for the expansion of gases. For the investigator to catch a bus could not add to the meaning of the formula. But if he were to experience an explosion, it might. But in the instance I have given, the realization—my patient's accident—did not approximate to the theory. It did not falsify it either. What is required is a realization that does approximate to the theory. From a sane point of view, or what is generally known as such, the patient is unlikely to find, in the world of external reality, any realization that approximates sufficiently to his statement to constitute meaning; there is nothing that will mate with his pre-conception to produce a conception. Therefore there cannot be any development such as is represented by the vertical axis of the Grid. But in the world of psychic reality there are realizations that approximate to the patient's statement.

This fact, recognized by psycho-analysts since Freud made his discoveries, is not taken sufficiently into account by the scientist who considers that a single negative fact can invalidate the theory it appears to contradict. Such an attitude to theory ignores its significance as a factor of mental growth. I stress the point because for the analyst it is essential to recognize this quality of the statement. The fact that a statement, and any scientific theory, can be matched by a realization in the domain of psychic reality is ignored by the natural scientist because it is in the world of physical realizations that he seeks his approximation, and because he fears and dislikes, with varying degrees of intensity, the existence of an approximate realization in the realm of psychic reality. This was, with reservations, true of my patient.

My patient's statement, his account of the episode and his display of feeling about it, required an interpretation from me. Briefly, a part of the interpretation was that he thought he was a puff of flatus. I attempted to make clear that his associations indicated the presence of a fantasy that he was a puff of flatus. As far as I could tell, there were two main obstacles to his understanding of this: first, it involved recognition of a domain that he feared, and second, that if he recognized the realization (his fantasy) as a realization that corresponded to his statement, others including myself would consider him mad.

Obviously this has substance, for an outside observer if he accepted the statement would not expect external reality to provide a realization that approximated to the statement, but would conclude that the explanation of the patient's statement was that the patient was mad. But, ignoring these obstacles, another problem now arises.

If the statement that the patient is a puff of flatus has as its approximating realization a fantasy that he is a puff of flatus, a logical construction that is a circular argument has come into being. It is similar to another argument that was typical of him. It would emerge that he was angry: he was angry because he was depressed. Why was he depressed? Obviously (in his view) because he was angry. And so on. I shall therefore consider the circular argument before taking up further details of this episode.

Experience of the circular argument, of which I have had a considerable amount, has convinced me that there is not much wrong with its logic, that it involves acceptance of a theory of causation, and that probably any logical argument is essentially circular. Since I am disposed to believe this of even classical instances of logical inquiry, I felt that the failures of circular arguments, such as those of my patient, to lead to any development had to be sought elsewhere than in their circularity. I decided that the difficulties that arose depended (to extend the use of the circle as a model) on the diameter. If the circular argument has a large enough diameter, its circular character is not detected and may, for all I know, contribute to useful discoveries such as I understand the curvature in space to be. But the curvature in space, in so far as I am able to understand it, provides me with a model for the postulate of a circular argument of such large diameter that it is conducive to the development of thought and personality. Conversely, the diameter can be so reduced that the circle itself disappears and only a point remains. Similarly with the circular argument. Restating this in the instance of my patient, the circular argument ends in the point (it may not be frivolous to say 'in the point of the argument') that he *is* a puff of flatus.

I shall try to make this statement clearer by returning to the patient and giving some details of what happens if the argument is not diminished in this way.

In my paper on thinking at the Edinburgh Conference (1962a), I pointed out the relationship of a 'thought' to a 'no-breast'. The thought owes its genesis to the absence of the object. I cannot enter into the bearing of this on the negative nature of a definition for lack of time but must point out that the statement, as the element that binds together a constant conjunction, at the same time implies that the constant conjunction is *not* any one of the constant conjunctions already bound.

In some instances the 'no-breast' is indicated, as it were, geometrically. That is to say, the mathematical counterpart of a thought is a point, something that marks the place where the breast was. Similarly, a line marks the place where the penis was—the 'no-penis'. The successive attacks on the breast, the 'no-breast', the thought (the place where the breast was) are repeated in the more complex combination of thoughts logically combined to form an argument. We thus witness the reduction of the fruitful, growth-producing circular argument, by the successive diminutions of 'diameter', until it becomes the sterile circular argument, of which the 'diameter' is further diminished until the circle disappears and only a point remains.

Does the statement 'circular argument' represent more than an element that can be categorized in a compartment of Row C? On the answer to this depends the usefulness of extending the model to include ideas of diameter. As I am not writing a clinical paper, I must limit clinical material to illustrations; I prefer, therefore, that the reader should not attach importance to them as anything other than models—part of my private thinking, which I hope may nonetheless serve for public communication.

A week or ten days elapsed after the episode of the accident had been produced in analysis. The time was taken up with many interpretations, including attempts to draw his attention to the circular argument. I did not say it was of small diameter, but I had this in mind myself. I was also able to show him his fear of any interpretation that drew his attention to the fact that he had two dissimilar views about the same facts. The interpretations were not new but appeared to produce a response in him. His statements continued to be remarkable more for their distance from any point (I mean this to be understood by the reader as a conversationally loose phrase) than for any attempt to get to grips with the point. Or (I now employ my model) he was engaged in a circular argument, the diameter being determined by the need to say nothing that brought him nearer the centre of the circle.

Then, not having directly referred to the episode again after his first mention of it, he said the car driver had called him a fucking fool. I feel better now, he said. I regarded this as meaning that his circular progress had brought him round to the point on the circle that was 'opposite' the statement that the car had collided with him. In time, at least, the argument was a circle of measurable diameter. But during that period of circular argument we had had opportunity for a number of interpretations, including the interpretation that he felt he was a puff of flatus. I therefore said that he felt the car accident was a sexual intercourse between a puff of flatus and the car and its driver. He said he felt better and added he felt he was going mad.

The point I wish to illustrate is that the circular argument of small diameter, though it precludes the matching or correlation of two statements and is therefore sterile, is preferred to the argument in a circle of relatively wide diameter because of the risk of a matching of two ideas that is accompanied by a feeling of madness. There is implicit in this the possibility that there must be distance between the correlated statements if meaning is to be achieved. If 'madness' is feared, the operation that leads to meaning is avoided. The circular argument must therefore be of small diameter to preclude the conjunction of meaning and a feeling of madness.

By my illustration I have intended briefly to indicate the value of considering the phenomena of psycho-analysis as statements (= transformations) that can be assessed by reference to Grid categories. My contention is that accuracy of observations is increased and that they are thereby brought into closer approximation to psycho-analytical theory. The gap between the events of an analysis and their interpretation consequently becomes easier to bridge.

In conclusion I shall refer briefly to the psycho-analytical game. Suppose, in the course of reviewing some aspect of the day's work, the analyst is satisfied that the interpretations he gave were adjusted with a reasonable degree of accuracy to the needs of the material. He may compare the categories to which he has assigned the patient's statements with the categories to which he would assign his interpretations. From this he may proceed to consider the nature of the relationship between material and interpretation. But he may also arbitrarily assign either interpretation or patients' statements to some different category and attempt to work out the implications of the arbitrary categorization. For example, he can place an interpretation that he is satisfied was correct in a Column 2 category such as D2 and then ask himself what the interpretation, correct though it may be, would be excluding. The analyst can set himself similar exercises not as a mere tax on his ingenuity but as a method of exercising and developing his capacity for intuition.

UNTITLED

Introduction

The following pages are transcripts I made from two tapes recorded by Bion sitting alone in his study, thinking of his forthcoming visit to Rome in July, 1977, to give talks and hold seminars. (Those seminars were published in Italian by Borla in 1983, under the title, *Seminari Italiani*.)

He speaks in a relaxed, reflective, meditative way, though it is clear that he is not talking to himself but to an imaginary, attentive audience. He sees himself 'idling away my time', thinking in an 'almost thoughtless' way, and then looking to see what he has caught in 'the net of my idleness'. But these verbal cogitations are far from the lazy meanderings of a day-dreamer; they are clear, sharp, and disciplined and tinged with his individual quirky sense of humour. Wild thoughts are domesticated, and stray thoughts are found a home.

The themes are all familiar ones to be found elsewhere in his writings, but he seldom repeated himself word for word; there are variations, expansions, additions, and some vivid meta-phorical passages.

Only minor editorial changes and corrections have been made, mostly with ease of reading in mind. Both days' recordings ended in mid-sentence; the tape ran out, not the speaker.

F.B.

28 May 1977

I f a thought without a thinker comes along, it may be what is a 'stray thought', or it could be a thought with the owner's name and address upon it, or it could be a 'wild thought'. The problem, should such a thought come along, is what to do with it. Of course, if it is wild, you might try to domesticate it. I shall consider later how you might try to do that. If its owner's name and address is attached, it could be restored to its owner, or the owner could be told that you had it and he could collect it any time he felt inclined. Or, of course, you could purloin it and hope either that the owner would forget it, or that he would not notice the theft and you could keep the idea all to yourself. If the owner is prepared to allow you to have it, or if it was understood that you were quite entitled to keep it, then you might try to train it in the way it should go and in a manner that would make it more amenable to the habits of your own resident thoughts and to the thoughts of the community of which you were a member, in such a way that it would gradually become assimilated and part and parcel of the totality of the group or person in whom the thought is to continue its existence.

What I am concerned with at the moment is the wild thoughts that turn up and for which there is no possibility of being able to trace immediately any kind of ownership or even any sort of way of being aware of the genealogy of that particular thought.

First of all, it seems to me to be simplest to try to tackle the problem by considering what this strange thought is. We might get a clue to it by wondering in what frame of mind or in what conditions this wild thought turned up and became enmeshed in our method of thinking. It could be that it seemed to occur to us when we were asleep. I am using this expression, 'when we were asleep', because it is a state of mind with which most people think they are familiar, so we can start with this somewhat familiar idea.

I want to consider the peculiar state of mind in which we are when we are asleep or, as is also frequently said and which has even become commonplace of psycho-analytic thinking, when we are unconscious, meaning by that when we are in a state in which we are not aware of our thoughts and feelings—or not quite. There are also some peculiar events that take place when we are asleep which are notorious and which are historically known to us, both in our private histories and in the history of the race. They are often said to be dreams. But I think it is as well to consider that it might be much more compatible with the events that take place if we could say to a person who reports that he has not been any-where but has been in bed and has slept well and so on, that what we would really like to know is where he went and what he saw during those hours when, according to him now, he was asleep. It is more than likely that he would reiterate that he went nowhere—he simply went to bed. But it is possible that he might also say: 'Well, of course, I had a dream—but then, it was only a dream.'

Freud was one of these peculiar people who seemed to think that dreams are worthy of further consideration. This has often happened. In the Book of Genesis dreams have been reported, including what are supposed to be interpretations of those dreams. There are other similarly well-known reported events, for example in the Book of Daniel, in which actual figures have been reported—mina, mina, and half minas—which seem to be straight-forward enough because they are applicable to weights and measures. However, there was something about them that led the dreamer—namely the person who picked up what I call this 'stray thought'—to feel that these words had some other meaning than the obvious one. Why he should think so, I don't know, and we never shall. But he actually found somebody who appeared to fall in with his idea and who gave the words an interpretation that, so it is said, turned out to be correct.

I want to leave it aside for a moment and not consider that matter any further than just to remind you of the existence of this peculiar state of mind where we see things and go to places which, when our state of mind changes because we happen to do what we call 'wake up', then we ignore these facts, these journeys, these sights, on the grounds that they are only dreams.

In case one of these strays comes along, I think I shall try to be prepared for its reception by arranging certain categories that might be suitable for placing the stray in a temporary—what? It is difficult to find the word for it. I do not find that the vocabulary that is available to me is very suitable for the purposes for which I want it just now, so I am going to call it a 'box'. The first box I am thinking of is really not suitable for anything so ephemeral as what I usually call a thought, namely, something that is physical; I shall call it a 'beta-element'. I don't know what that means and I don't know what it is, and as it hasn't turned up I am still ignorant. But anyway, there it is, in case that strange creature should exist and should it swim into my ken.

There is something a bit more sophisticated: that is to say a similarly physical creature, but one that arouses in me primordial thoughts or feelings, something that is a sort of prototype of a mental reaction. These I shall call 'alpha-elements'. I likewise don't know much about them, but I think I have been in states of mind in which I am aware of their existence. That is to say, I have what I call a stomach ache or a headache, or I am possibly told that I have been extremely restless and have been tossing and turning around. I remember this on an occasion in which I was amused to hear that in the school sanatorium I had been in a state that was really rather impressive; I was told I had been delirious after an accident. That gained me a certain prestige amongst my fellows that I had been so seriously ill. During this stage I had actually picked up a chair and hurled it across the room—luckily not hitting anybody.

There have also been these occasions when I have again fallen into the prevalent idea of saying that I had a dream, but I can only say that I felt physical pain—my arm ached; I even had some kind of reminiscence after waking up that my arm was stiff. That is the kind of thing, should it turn up, that I should like to put in this category.

There is another one in which I am nearly awake and nearly asleep; there I have certain ideas that are comprehensible to me when I am fully awake and of which I can tell you exactly in terms of verbal formulations of visual images what I say I dreamt or saw in my sleep. By this time I think I could consider that I am in a different state of mind, namely a conscious or waking frame of mind. Again I am in difficulties because I don't in fact know what to call it, but perhaps you might be able to grasp my meaning. Perhaps it would be better at this stage if I took the precaution of going back again and resorting to numbers, calling the beta-elements 1, the alpha-elements 2; these pictorial images and so forth I could put into the category of 3, or C. It could be A, B, C; 1, 2, 3, and then D4, E5, F, G, H. . . . Becoming wider and wider awake, I hesitate, because I would like at the same time to have these boxes available for rather different, or apparently different, creatures, so that I could consider what could be called, math-ematically, the negative versions of it. They could be marked H–, G–, F–, E–, etc. down to zero (0). In that kind of way one has room for quite a zoo, quite a number of strays and thoughts without owners or with owners . . . [*a temporary break in recording*]

The advantage of what I have said so far is that I think I can put this down, record it on a piece of paper on which I could make the appropriate marks. I can try to communicate it to you.

Thinking it over, I find I am somewhat dissatisfied, and although I also feel it is very unlikely that I shall ever be satisfied, I will attempt to put my dissatisfaction to some good purpose by considering one or two other possible methods of making pro-vision for these strays.

It occurs to me that, in case they become visible to me, I might be able to put them into the appropriate colour; for example, tak-ing the cue from dreams that I have had, colours like the blue of the sky, the red of blood, and the yellow of ochre, the colour that is made out of earth. They are primitive colours, these primary col-ours, and they might be very useful. When it comes to this sort of thing which I have called a beta-element, it gets more difficult; I don't know what to call that. Perhaps, provisionally it would do to say, 'gross darkness', which is different from darkness, which has a certain amount of light in it; this would be with absolutely no light whatsoever, the sort of light verbalized by Victor Hugo as '*le néant*', or by Shakespeare [*Macbeth*, V. iii] when he talks about 'a tale told by an idiot, full of sound and fury, signifying nothing'— zero, 0. I am not very happy about it because, thinking of it in a somewhat linear manner, I would like to start with these positive numbers and letters down to minus 1, 2, 3, 4, indefinitely. I think it would lead to infra-red and ultra-violet. If it were the numerological categorization, there I would have to use some term like 'infinity'. The worst of not being a mathematician or an artist is that I am very much in the position of the infant or foetus, which, I imagine, hasn't adequate modes of expression or communication, and in many ways hasn't a great deal to communicate. I suppose the infant might want to communicate that it was either lonely or hungry. And I, in this peculiar world in which I now find myself, am both in need of nourishment and of somebody with whom to communicate, not because I have an awful lot to say, but because I find myself in the state of mind with which I am distressingly familiar—the state of mind in which I can only say I am abysmally, literally and metaphorically, ignorant. That is one reason why it is a matter of some urgency to me to be able to find some sort of network in which I can catch any thoughts that are available.

I think you can see I am already finding myself in difficulties, so I would like again to pick up some further tentative categorization that would be suitable for any thoughts. The nearest I can get to it is probably the sort of thing the musicians know about and have developed very successfully. I remember seeing some kind of animal in a zoo when I was very small: it was rattling its horns on the bars of the enclosure. The peculiar thing about this creature was that it kept on entirely rhythmically. It was most extraordinary, so much so that I was able to draw the attention of a grown-up who was with me, who was himself a very perceptive man, and he agreed that this was remarkably and clearly an established rhythm that could be written down.

I am still stirred by these rhythmical communications. It is fascinating to hear a group of drummers performing; it has the same sort of effect upon me as is described by a poet when he talks about 'the brave music of a distant drum' (*The Rubáiyát of Omar Khayyám*, Fitzgerald, 1859, p. xii). I remember in war being incredibly moved when I heard the distant music of the bagpipes of a Highland division that was to accompany us in battle. I have heard many different kinds of music since then, including that described by Osbert Lancaster as betraying the presence of the English army, namely, 'snatches of tuneless song'. When I first heard Stravinsky's music to Petrouchka, I thought it was somewhat incomprehensible and not very pleasing, but very sophisticated. I shall have occasion to refer to this again later on.

I have been idling away my time, thinking in this way—a way I could describe as being almost thoughtless. If, as a child, I had been caught at it, somebody would have said, 'Why on earth don't you find something to do?' I would now like to have a look in case I have caught anything in the net of my idleness.

What is this first specimen? 'Golden boys and girls all must, like chimney-sweepers, come to dust.' This stray has a name and address attached to it—Shakespeare. ('Golden lads and girls all must, / As chimney-sweepers, come to dust': *Cymbeline*, IV. ii.) The only address I know is Stratford-upon-Avon, but I gather he is dead anyway, so I'll adopt this piece of property that is in fact his.

I am afraid it seems terribly hackneyed to me. It is one of these things about which I could say, 'Yes I know . . . yes I know', words I have learnt to regard with great suspicion and sadness. Whenever I hear the expression, 'Yes I know' or 'You know', repeated again and again, I find myself feeling sad, because I feel that it is going to be very difficult to get to, or to communicate, what I want to know or communicate—there's hardly room for it because everybody knows, including myself. It is almost an archaeological operation to excavate this knowledge in the hopes of finding a thought buried somewhere inside it, possibly even some wisdom.

In a way this is rather like experiences I have in psycho-analytic sessions. Patients who come to me have nearly all heard everything I have to say; they have read it in books, they have heard about psycho-analysts and psychiatrists and even cures. What they have to say to me is also deeply buried because they have become so used to saying it and knowing that it is a complete waste of time trying to find anybody who will listen to what they are saying.

The sort of excavation that would seem to be required to get through to a little bit of wisdom is so intimidating that one feels nothing short of a spade or a shovel, or nowadays even an atomic bomb, would ever get through to it. However, although I am sure that these forcible means of communication might sometimes expose something valuable, I don't think that I would advocate atomic explosion as a mode of archaeological exploration of the Ziggurat. As a matter of fact even extremely knowledgeable, wise people like Sir Arthur Evans [have been accused of being destructive] on the grounds that they have destroyed more than they have illuminated by their excavations and re-constructions. Just as the archaeologist has to be very careful when he thinks he has reached some potentially revealing object and has to resort not to a spade or a shovel but a camel-hair brush, so the analyst has to know when to discard these crude and violent methods and when to pick up something far gentler, far more revealing and less destructive than a shovel. It is difficult to know—and this is one, and only one, reason—why psycho-analysis needs to be carefully done, because the situation is so precarious and because it is so difficult to find the minimum conditions for achieving wisdom either in oneself or in one's collaborator—namely the patient.

Let's go back to the find—'Golden boys and girls all must like chimney-sweepers come to dust', together with, 'Yes I know, we all know that, and probably we are as sick to death of it as we are of other chunks of Shakespeare we have picked up in our time, or been forced to learn at school'.

Hugh Kenner, by accident overhearing a Warwickshire yokel talking, discovered the further meaning, probably current in Shakespeare's time: 'golden boys and girls' could refer to the dandelion, which, when the petals have dropped, looks like a chimney-sweep's broom and is then known as a 'chimney-sweeper'. So from that point of view Shakespeare is able to use a simple phrase and simple language, which then communicates an idea hundreds of years later to people who have probably forgotten entirely the commonplace meaning of the words he used originally and which were commonplace when he used them, and transformed them into immortal phrases that last for hundreds of years and take their meaning with them. A similar state of affairs is produced by him over and over again, as we all know. 'The raven himself is hoarse that croakes the fatal entrance of Duncan under my battlements' [*Macbeth*, I. v]. The most difficult and longest word in that sentence is 'battlements', and yet the total sentence conveys a meaning which is extremely depth-stirring and provokes profound feelings. What, then, is the language, the method of communication, that we are to employ when we want to describe, or when we want to formulate or capture, as it were, an idea that comes to us, maybe that is communicated by somebody else, but maybe comes to us in our dreams or in frames of mind with which we are not familiar whether we are awake or asleep?

What I want to express is some kind of experience that we are able to have if we are psycho-analysts and concerned with that area of thought. You might ask, what area of thought? We have to use words like 'psycho-analysis'—they are long words, ugly words, impressive words, and words that are devoid of meaning. I can only say, 'You have to have an analysis to know what I am talking about, or you have to be an analyst', which is very unsatisfactory if I wish to communicate it or pass it on. We think that the analytic experience, the real thing, the basic thing, the fundamental thing, is worth preserving and therefore worth communicating to people next week, next year, next century, and perhaps three or four hundred years later—not in order to inform them, but in order to let them see the sort of path of thought or being that stretched out in front of us, and will stretch out in front of us probably for a long time if there are any of us to see it. 'They closed the road through the woods many years ago'—the ending of the poem where Kipling describes the sound of the horses galloping through the woods. ['They shut the road through the woods / Seventy years ago.'—'The Way through the Woods'.] We can talk about the woods that still exist, using the term metaphorically, meaning it as a method of talking about what we are concerned with now, tomorrow, and all the tomorrows, because the road through the woods is obscured by the trees and can even be obscured by the woods that spring up, so we are concerned with a very peculiar form of excavation. We occasionally come across a child who cannot learn the alphabet. Usually antagonism is aroused in the teacher because the child is so stupid, but it is forgotten that for many reasons the child may not see or understand why it should learn the alphabet. After all, I am familiar with the situation in which we have patients who cannot see the words for the alphabet, who cannot see the sentences for the words, and who certainly cannot see the spirit of man lurking somewhere behind this plentiful crop of jargon or verbal weeds that proliferate at an extraordinary pace, and in some climates flourish in such a way that it is difficult to believe there is any meaning in psycho-analysis whatsoever.

Freud was extremely impressed with Charcot's statement that when you do not understand a situation, when you cannot perceive what the diagnosis is, you should go on until the obscurity begins to be penetrated by a pattern, and then you can formulate what the pattern is that you see. With regard to ourselves, we are confronted with what seems to be a single individual. Our attention is usually focused on a recently developed capacity of the human being, namely his capacity to elaborate and use articulate speech. It is obviously a very powerful and useful achievement. But while we are in the frame of mind in which it is possible to command the use of relatively recently developed techniques like articulate speech, we also have to contend with the many obscuring words, thoughts, sounds, physical feelings, physical symptoms, in order to excavate the underlying, basic, and fundamental feature. Not so long ago doctors were very satisfied to detect the fact that a patient was suffering from a disease known as dropsy. Having detected the disease known as dropsy, they find there isn't one: there are all sorts of diseases—heart failure and so forth. It is very discouraging in spite of the gratification that can be obtained by apparently getting that much nearer to the origin. What about the man or woman who presents himself in your office? This person is the most powerful, knowledgeable collaborator you are ever likely to find. In this lonely job one has to do all by oneself, alone, although at the same time in the room with somebody else, that 'somebody' is both the person who presents himself for assistance and the person to whom we look for the most powerful assistance we are ever likely to find.

If we are concerned with physical disease, we have to learn the language the body talks; we can look at the expression, the ruddy blush of health, 'rude' health, and distinguish that from an obscure blood disease, and so on. The human animal, unlike other species, can lie and has probably had a good deal of practice at lying and misinforming from a very early stage, because feelings of guilt precipitate a proliferation of a capacity to lie and deceive—both the person himself and whoever else might be able to detect the supposed crime that the infant does not know about, although the infant can show any amount of guilt. The question is, then, what is the mental counterpart of these lies, these statements, this deceiving blush of rude health, this appearance of athletic somatic health and capacity, the apparent facility with which a male body can display erectile tissue? Many people have been taken in by supposing that the boy or man is both potent because he has a penis and because it can become visibly erect. This is much more hidden with the woman in whom it may be more difficult to detect any signs of erection, but psychologically she may be very potent, much more potent than the boy or man to whom she looks, and from whom she expects sexual potency. We all know situations in which mothers have been shocked and frightened at discovering that their babies can cause their nipples to become erect and so find it difficult to feed the baby; the infant finds it difficult also to participate in the feeding because of the mother's dread of these peculiar sensations, which can also be aroused by supposing that the feeding baby itself shows signs of erection. Those are all physical—what the psychological or mental counterpart of it is I don't know. That is one reason why I think it is useful to consider keeping this box into which I propose to put my various beta-elements, situations that are not really thoughts and about which it is easier for me to say, 'I think I know what this patient is thinking, but I am jolly sure they would say they weren't—if they were thinking at all.'

To return to a point I have already mentioned—I could say to a patient, 'where were you last night and what did you see?' and they say they went nowhere and saw nothing—they were asleep, asleep in bed, and can hotly deny that they went anywhere or saw anything. I can see that if you restrict your vision or your topic of conversation or discussion to geographical movement, then it would be perfectly true that there are many places that could be said not to have been visited. What does Mandalay look like? Or Pondicherri? Or Samarkand? Or Jerusalem? Some people might give a description of it—they know what it looks like; they have travelled so much and know so much about these places and others like them that they cannot really answer my question.

What does 'sex' mean? What does 'Oedipus situation' mean? Look it up, if possible, in the position in which there are only two people, namely the analyst and the analysand. Where would you locate this story? And anyhow, what is the story? You can look it up in the mythological dictionary, if you like. I don't know why the Sphinx is so often not mentioned. Perhaps it is because the Sphinx committed suicide and we don't know whether to exercise our curiosity or whether to kill it off. We are so familiar with psycho-analytic theories that we tend to forget the basic points; so much so, that it is difficult to say what the fundamental points are. Free associations—sometimes we hear of analysis in such a way that we think what a wonderful time we are all having, wandering about amongst the weeds, plucking the wild and beautiful flowers, admiring the brambles, the bushes, and not getting anywhere near to disturbing the sleep of the sleeping beauty—the wisdom that lies fast asleep somewhere in the thickets; somewhere buried, not only literally under the mounds of the Ziggurat or the site of Ur of the Chaldees or Knossos, but what about the Oracle at Delphi? Is that voice in any way audible? Does this sound very romanticized when it comes to a question of Doctor X and this tiresome woman, or perverse man, to suppose that somewhere buried beneath these accumulations of knowledge there is some spark of wisdom that could still be blown into a flame? There are always people who say, 'Yes it can. Don't do it. If you blow the sparks into a flame, you will start a conflagration, and goodness knows where that will end—don't do it.' There are plenty of people who still will say, 'The world was all right till these awful Freudians and Kleinians came to it. They are the people who are responsible for all this sexual promiscuity and general disorder.' As Freud himself pointed out, there is nothing new about the situation where people complain about doctors as always discovering and inventing new diseases and illnesses—they have a vested interest in doing so because, after all, they can get paid for curing them. There is a certain plausibility in it; there is plenty of room for corruption, dishonesty, fraud, but even so I think there is something to be said for what we call 'medical science'. These terms like 'science' are so debased; they are like coins in which the denomination is impossible to detect because it has been worn so smooth that it is no longer possible to distinguish the design that was originally marked upon it and that made it comprehensible.

What I want to do is to indicate the sort of area with which we are all concerned. Later I hope to consider how we are to turn our concern into activity that is worth while.

For the present we have to consider which of our capacities are of any value in this particular regard. We do not in fact know who the person is today, tomorrow, with whom we are meeting. What we already know and what the patient already knows is of no consequence or importance; the past is past, and anyhow that term is part of the convenience of articulate expression. The reason why we concern ourselves with things that are remembered, with our past history, is not because of what it was—although that might be quite important in its own right—but because of the mark it has left on you or me or us *now*. In what way are any of these things detectable? The embryologists say we can detect remains of a vestigial tail, branchial clefts, etc., seeming to suggest a fishy origin of a very primitive kind from which we have diverged. But if that is the case physically, I think it is possible that it might also be mentally; there might still be traces in the mind or character or the personality, *in the present*, of particles that have a long history, things that we would expect to be fundamental, basic, primordial.

Do any of these remnants betray themselves in what we can now observe in the human speech of the person we are talking to, as well as in ourselves who are doing the talking? That is what seems to me to be one of the fundamental discoveries of psychoanalysis: archaic states of mind, archaic thoughts and ideas, primitive patterns of behaviour are all detectable in the most civilized, cultivated people; in more primitive people we would expect them to be less hidden. These archaic elements may turn out to be of some consequence today; suppose, for example, that the remnants of a branchial cleft could develop into a branchial cleft tumour. In this way there can be certain detectable archaic elements in our personalities or minds, which are really survivals and which are capable of proliferating in a beneficent manner, but also in a cancerous manner, a pathological manner. That is the only reason why it seems to me to be interesting to be seeing a patient today and tomorrow and in the future if he or she will submit to being observed again and also . . . [*tape ends*]

29 May 1977

Anybody reading this account so far in the first chapter can see that it is hardly what you would describe as 'scientific'; that is to say, it could be seen as something that, according to the individual who is reading it, can be assessed as imaginative, or fanciful, or imitation science. It is a matter of opinion. I mention this point because these opinions have to be entertained when one is attempting to evaluate—whatever it is: whether it is the physical appearance of a person, or whether it is his character that seems to be betrayed in what he says or writes or does. In short, we are making a kind of interpretation of what evidence is brought into us by our senses. There is still the fact that it would be helpful to know what the quality of the information is which is brought in, because we depend on evaluating that evidence. First of all we have to evaluate the value of the actual gathering mechanism. I, for example, have now a good deal of experience on which to base my opinion about how reliable I would consider my impressions to be, and how healthy I consider my ability to see, how accurately my eyes work, and so on.

Although it is possible to divide this discussion up when it is a question of talking or writing, making these verbal transformations, we cannot in fact divide up whatever it is we are in contact with and which we wish to assess and to understand; that is not divided up, not even in any way, although I suppose you could say you 'heard' it, or 'saw' it, or you heard somebody 'say' it. Those divisions are more applicable to the machinery, the personality and its equipment, which is gathering the information, than it is to the universe in which we exist. The universe does not obey the laws of articulate speech, or the laws of optics, although we consider that the laws are approximating to light itself. But it is questionable how much of the laws apply to the actual objective phenomena and to what extent the laws only apply to, or are

39

largely significant of, the human capacities. We shall see later that this is true of a number of different activities that we can talk about in the sense of our logical capacity as well as our capacity to feel and think and observe.

This introduction is itself a pause in which I am attempting to evaluate what I have already said in the process of continuing to talk, to think about this subject.

I am not really attempting to assess the nature of the information that is brought to me by my physical senses, what I would call the beta-elements, material that seems to be more physical than mental. I know nothing about it. I merely suppose that it exists; I merely suppose that it is on a structure of that kind that I have built up the whole system, architectonics of thought. So I shall go on from this point, which I could describe as an operation of curiosity, a fact-gathering tendency, to the nature of the facts I gather, and then to the communication of such information as I consider my activities have gleaned.

The point at which I am starting is what I could call speculative imagination and speculative reasoning. I would like to divide the two for the moment into categories that I could describe, borrowing from mathematics, as sub-sets of a main set.

First, I would consider speculative imagination. What sort of value is to be attributed to that? My own impression is that it is very important. When I have attempted to supervise people who want to come to me for analytic supervision—part of a learning activity—I suggest they should not bother very much about what I or anybody else might think about their contributions, but should proceed to say what their interpretation is of the material they have told me. I find they are invariably very suspicious and very anxious to give an interpretation that has the blessing of some psycho-analytic authority, or that they think I might approve of if I were a psycho-analytic authority of sufficient importance and consequence. I won't bother to consider the nature of that authority, because I know quite enough about myself to regard the tendency to believe that I am a psychoanalytic authority as very misleading indeed and obstructive to progress. I stress this point: 'Please say what you like; please say what you think or imagine is the meaning of what you have told me.' The reason why I say this is not because I am suggesting that all you have to do is to disconnect

your mind from your jaw and allow your jaw and your tongue to
waggle. That is not my idea, but I think it is a preliminary; even
before we are able to think very much, or have enough capacity to
be able to think, we should learn to be able to let our tongue and
our jaw waggle, as I put it; even if it doesn't make much sense, it
may be a step on the way to articulate speech. Similarly, these
speculative imaginations, however ridiculous, however neurotic,
however psychotic, may nevertheless be stages on the way to what
we would ultimately regard as scientific, psycho-analytic formulations. This idea may be quite erroneous, but I put it forward
because you can test it for yourselves and come to your own conclusions. From my experience it seems to be very important. When
you have, as honestly as you can, allowed your imagination to play
on the material and allowed yourself to state it in such terms as
you can, then you can assess the nature of the product. I would
say, therefore, that it is a good thing to say what you think you
have seen. Never mind what your state of mind is; let's forget all
that, let's have respect for the information that you gather in that
state of mind, no matter what it is—whether it is a state of mind
that subsequently you can assess by saying you dreamt it, or you
hallucinated it, or you just painted it, or you 'doodled' it onto a
piece of paper when you weren't thinking about anything in particular, or that you might, if you were gifted in that way, actually
compose it or play a tune or whistle or sing it. I have heard people
say it is useful for a stammerer to try singing, and then he becomes
able to articulate in the ordinary manner. I regard speculative
imagination as worthy of concern—never mind whether you
dreamt it, hallucinated it, or whether it is an object of delusion,
or—I don't know what a drawing or painting is the product of. I
take it that presumably the artist saw or thought he saw what he
has drawn. If we consider renaissance art, for example, we can see
plenty of pictures of saints, crucifixions, adorations; when did they
see them? And how could they see them so clearly that they could
even put a line around them and give them colour and form in
such a way that I can look at one of those things now and say, 'This
man saw this three hundred, four hundred, four thousand years
ago'. Or I was able to walk into the Lascaux caves and see on the
walls various marks and signs of painting and drawing—somewhat distorted, it is true, because I see them with the aid of electric

lighting, which reveals very clearly their shape and colour. I don't know what sort of light they were seen in when they were drawn. Similarly, I can walk into the Elephantine caves near Bombay and once again see the carvings that were made; again, I do not know in what light or in what frame of mind. I guess that my frame of mind is rather different from the frame of mind of the artist who painted them, in much the same way as I *think* I can understand the verbal formulations of a Shakespeare play—at least I am helped to do so if I can get very capable actors who know how to translate a printed drama into the dramatic form. I say this because I think it is sometimes forgotten that nowadays we are already dependent on fine performances, even of a Shakespeare play, before we can say we really understand it. It depends very much on being able to trust the evidence of our senses, on being able to depend on the actors to make the play comprehensible. I have quoted *Cymbeline*: 'Golden boys and girls all must, like chimney-sweepers, come to dust.' I have to interpret that in a state of mind that is, three or four hundred years later, fully conscious, when I am wide awake; it is quite different from that state of mind of the person who wrote those lines originally. I do not know what the state of mind was; I do not know what the English was that was spoken in Warwickshire at that time. I can only marvel at the product of a state of mind like that, as I can marvel at the state of mind of a Leonardo who sees Saint Ann, the Virgin Mary, and can see them so clearly. The best I can do is to make myself available to learn whatever it is that they might have been able to communicate when they were alive and of which they have left a record that I can still see or hear for myself.

This somewhat long-winded description is to draw attention to the fact that when you see your patient tomorrow, I do not know whom you will see and nor do you. It might be anybody. I am sure we have to have respect for that mind or personality; that seems to me to be the most valuable thing about the whole of psycho-analysis—the suggestion that the human mind and its products are worthy of attention. I am not suggesting you are going to see William Shakespeare; I am not suggesting you are going to see the writer of the *Baghavad Gita* or some famous painter or sculptor or composer, a Mozart—we don't know. But I do suggest that you will not know unless you are able to respect the actual experience made available to you when the patient goes so far as to spend time and money coming to see you. If you are not dealing with somebody who is worth all that scrutiny, all I can say is, it is possible that it may be worth while if we ourselves are sufficiently worthwhile to be capable of learning something from the experience. So there is always a chance that the engagements you and I have made for the morrow could be turned to good account. It may turn out to be very worthwhile because the patient is a person of some importance or consequence and has gifts that have so far not been revealed or, if they have been revealed, have been dismissed on the grounds that he or she is stupid, or psychotic, or crazy. The same thing may apply, although it is now unlikely, to ourselves—unlikely because most of us have lived quite long enough for some sort of gift to have made itself manifest by this time. Let us hope that analysis has afforded us a chance, by becoming psycho-analysts, to betray such abilities as perchance we have. I am bound to say that I think it is a matter of optimism; I don't think a great deal of importance can be attached to any hope of that kind—not as far as I myself am concerned. But on the other hand I don't think that we should be obstructed either by hopes or fears. If hopes are dupes, fears may be liars ['If hopes were dupes, fears may be liars': Arthur Hugh Clough, 'Say Not the Struggle Naught Availeth']; so we have to have respect for ourselves and for the analysand.

The point is important because I find psycho-analysts have difficulty in realizing that there are minimum conditions necessary for the activity we call psycho-analysis. Some of those conditions lie within our own control; that is to say, we can avoid being in an unsuitable frame of mind; we can avoid being a prey to what I can most easily describe as a state of rhapsody, of being in such good humour that we allow all our emotions and wishes and desires full play. That is not much more use than it would be to arrive heavily drugged, literally with alcohol, or metaphorically with our optimism or pessimism or despair. In this respect it is therefore important to be rid of our memories and desires.

As regards supervision, it is a good thing not to look to the supervisor to give information or knowledge about psychoanalysis. In so far as it is possible to pick up an idea or two in a supervision, or even in analysis, it may be just as well to forget them when you are with the analysand because if you don't then, your mind can already be so filled with your wishes, desires, theories, expectations, that there simply isn't room for an idea; there are no interstices through which what is available to your senses can penetrate to your capacity to understand. I am not going to bother you at the moment with what this capacity to understand may be; that is another matter we have to consider later. It is something that has been discussed and debated for many centuries, even before psycho-analysis was ever heard of.

The analyst needs to be divested or denuded of his memories and his desires so as to leave room for him to be open to the present—what I call the present. Psycho-analysis gives the impression, by which I think we are liable to be misled, that what is important is the past. The past is not important, because you can do nothing about it; the only things about which you can do anything are the remnants, the vestiges of the past, of past states of mind or archaic parts of our physical make-up—the branchial clefts, the vestigial tail, etc., our simian ancestry—but it is possible to make use of these vestiges that are discernible in the present if we allow ourselves to discern them. Even physically it may be useful to have some kind of remnant of knowledge about embryology if we are trying to assess a patient who comes complaining of some tumour of the neck or other physical symptoms that have begun to obtrude.

Our position, as I see it, is that although we tend to have shifted our observations away from the body to the sphere of the mind, the body has not ceased to exist. Because we try to make use of the facts that the patient reports by turning them into what we call 'free associations' that we can then interpret, it doesn't mean that the facts weren't facts. Patients sometimes say, 'But isn't it reasonable for me to feel this when I told you what I have been seeing?' Of course I don't know whether it is reasonable or not—that is up to the patient. I am in no way doubting the accuracy, or that he is not sincere in believing that he has given me an accurate description of what he has seen, but I am disregarding those aspects of it because he knows more about it than I do. I am trying to look at something else, to hear something else, to be open to something else—vestiges, mental vestiges. I don't know where they come from; I don't know where the patient comes from. I don't mind whether he has given me his name and address and telephone number, because that is not of immediate consequence—it is important for obvious reasons, but because it is obvious it is not important—what is obvious is obvious, and there is nothing more to be said about it. The patient can have his own opinion of what he can see and know for himself; what is much more difficult for him is something he cannot see, and that is why he has come to me. Patients have difficulty in understanding that they have *not* come to me because they know the answer, in spite of the fact that we often hear people say, 'Yes I know . . . yes I know . . . yes I know', and 'Well, I knew that anyway'. That kind of statement is indicative, it is a sign, it is what we might call a symptom to which the analyst pays attention, not because there is any difficulty about the grammar or syntax being employed, but because it is revelatory, or could be potentially revelatory, of a state not so far discerned or of which the patient is not aware.

It is important that the embryo–analyst, the candidate, should dare to use his imagination and dare to try to articulate it in a supervision. That is one reason why I regard a supervision as being possibly valuable; if only those who come dare to say what they think and if only they will use that occasion as a way of practising trying to articulate what they think, either in verbal terminology, or if they find any other, I am perfectly happy. A patient once said to me, 'If you only had a piano here, I could play the thing to you; I can't talk like this to you.' If I could understand music, I should be very glad for him to do so, but here again, there are these minimum conditions that are necessary for analysis. After a time I begin to know what the minimum conditions are for *me* to do analysis. The same thing has to be determined by any other analyst. It is a great mistake for an analyst to lose sight of that fact. You can make concessions if you want to; you can relax your own rules if you want to—temporarily, at any rate—but that is a matter of opinion and a matter of judgement. But generally speaking, what you have to know is what your minimum conditions are. For example, the patient may think he has the right to drag you out of your chair, or to wrestle with you, or even sometimes to use firearms against you to make what you have to say inaudible. The analyst must be clear in his mind where he draws the line, where the minimum conditions for him to analyse have ceased to exist because they have been so eroded by denial. This crops up with a child who does not know how to behave in the analyst's room, and the child's parents very often don't know how to behave with regard to the analyst who is trying to analyse their child. But the analyst has to be very clear and quite firm in stating his minimum requirements, without which it becomes impossible for him to do analysis. That is the only reason for exerting a certain discipline; not because we want to prevent anybody from doing whatever they like; we don't even want them to come for analysis, necessarily. People are free to take up an analysis if they want to do so, but we are also obliged to say what are the conditions we have to have in order to be able to fulfil that aim.

The point we are discussing and to which this is relevant is this matter of speculative imagination. Unless the analyst allows himself the exercise of his speculative imagination he will not be able to produce the conditions in which the germ of a scientific idea can flourish. We have to bear in mind that even psycho-analysis itself is at the beginning of its career. It is only quite recently that the human race has learnt how . . . [*tape ends*]

There are many different kinds of language; some forms are hardly to be translated into articulate speech, because they are not really articulate forms of communication. Chinese, for example, has a great many hieroglyphic signs. Not only is it true of their language; I think there can be a conflict between, say, Chinese and Russians, although superficially there can be agreement, apparently, between their ideas of the way in which the human race should be governed. But the Chinese, with their hieroglyphic method of communication, also attach a lot of importance to the small muscles of the face and are prejudiced in favour of communications with people who allow themselves facial expression—muscular expression—when they talk. They don't like people whose faces are impassive. So there may be great agreement between the ideas of different races, but great differences that are not openly expressed because they are expressed in muscular ways, physical ways. In the famous guide book on Spain, Ford (1845, Vol. 1, p. 83) gives a good description of the gestures commonly employed—the gestures of the hand, etc. It is extremely informative and shows how much importance would be attached by two people, talking to each other, to what they say and how that is accompanied by movements of muscles—hands, face, etc.

The analyst has to be quite clear, or as near as he can get in the course of time, as to what are the minimum requirements on which he proposes to exist. For example, I feel that if anybody wants an analysis they will have to come to my consulting-room, because I have not the means by which I can get to theirs, or the time. It is not because that is a particularly good thing for the patient, it simply happens to be the limitation imposed on me by my own limitations. I have to say, 'I shall have to ask you, if you want to try this, to come to see me here at a particular time, for another session, or two more sessions.' But of course it is nothing like as simple as that; there are so many things which are not easily formulated, and it is not until you know what the patient is capable of in the way of communication, obstruction, hostility, that you can be quite clear whether you can stand it or whether you can't. The reason for discussing the matter at all is because you need to be prepared to say to the patient, 'thus far, and no further'—not because you want to stop him from doing anything he likes, but because you understand that he wants an analysis and you know whether or not you can do analysis in the conditions the patient is proposing.

On the way to being an analyst, you have to reserve the right to indulge your speculations, your speculative imagination. Perhaps you might want to sculpt, or paint, or draw, or compose music or fiction, in order to give your imagination an airing, to give it a chance to develop into something that might be scientific.

Another sub-set: speculative reason, similar to the other. Here again, you can give your reason for whatever it is. Reasons are extremely prolific, they flourish, they crop up like weeds. As I said earlier, they can be like brambles that proliferate so vigorously that they make cultivation impossible. This means that in the course of this speculative imagination, speculative reason, there is no particular reason to prevent—and I think every reason why we should not prevent—your speculation and your capacity for reason from exercising itself. But I think it should not be allowed for too long to be purely a sort of rhapsody, purely a state of affairs such as Valéry describes: it is imagined that the poet goes to sleep or indulges in a drunken orgy and wakes up to be able to write down a poem. He says that that is not the way in which poetry is written; in fact the poet has to be much nearer to being a mathematician. So while I say that it is extremely important to exercise your imagination, to let it go, to give it a chance to flourish, at the same time keep it under some sort of discipline.

At some point, while you are exercising your imagination, you are trying to imagine what sort of person this is that you are making contact with. When the person comes into your room, it may be possible to answer that question starting with the answer— the name and address and telephone number, etc., of that person. But you can go further than that; you can see whether it is a man or woman, tall or short, covered up by the clothes or revealed by them. You have to interpret the clothes worn, the manners displayed, and wonder, 'Can I imagine what a person is like who looks like X who has just walked into my room?' Could you ever have imagined that that person, who looks just like a man, existed? Or that that person who looks just like a man but has rouged cheeks, or is wearing sports clothes, could have existed? If you are frank, I think you have to admit you couldn't. The one thing that is really incredible is a fact. Conversely, when somebody comes into your room who looks just like anybody else, you still have to be able to retain your scepticism and say, 'Could anybody who looks just like anybody else possibly exist?' You have to believe your senses and say, 'Yes, apparently'. The facts are incredible, but don't be beguiled into believing them because they are facts.

What do you believe, then? When you know what you believe, then you might think it useful to communicate it to somebody who isn't you. I can believe that it might be useful to try to communicate to people who are not me what I think psycho-analysis is, or how I should be a psycho-analyst. I don't know that it is really possible, but it *is* possible that other people might get an idea of how I do psycho-analysis if they are given a chance to find out. They don't necessarily have to rely on what I say is how I do it— they can form their own opinion. Even when you are not sure about this matter of soul and super-soul, a super-ego, an id, and an atmen, perhaps you can come to some architectonic, some idea of how you would describe the structure of the personality as a by-product of what you see when a person comes into your consulting-room and says, ostensibly quite truthfully, that they want an analysis. Speculative imagination, speculative reasoning—to put into pictorial terms, a new-born infant opening its eyes and staring at its mother. Imagine it or pictorialize it as you wish.

What next? What stage would succeed that of a speculation and imaginative reconstruction of this kind? Possibly reconstruction has something to do with it; possibly we do attempt to formulate a kind of architectonic, the building-up of a system of thought into a stable form. I can think of various versions of it, like Cantor's exploration of matrices. We are familiar with Freud's attempt to build up a system; we are also familiar with the fact that he felt that he had not completed his investigation, that his life was not prolonged sufficiently for him to satisfy even himself that he had completed his system or what he was capable of. The problem has to be passed on, delegated to his survivors, the inheritance passes to others who might be called his professional family, his professional colleagues.

Recently even the mathematicians have considered theories like Heisenberg's Uncertainty Principle, the incompleteness theory; they indicate how the same awareness of incompleteness, uncertainty, has penetrated into things that have appeared to be so settled, so serviceable, such as mathematics, logic. Even a logical construction is criticized on logical grounds; this means that there is still some sort of logic but our understanding of logic has to extend—not that the logic is inadequate. This is what is happening with the Intuitionists—Brouwer, Heyting, etc.: they are investigating or proposing a mathematics that arouses a good deal of hostility on the part of the established mathematicians. In metapsychology Gödel's investigation, his theory about the Law of the Excluded Middle, also arouses curiosity. We could say that this exercise of curiosity, of speculation, extends even into the realms of speculation. To that extent we could say there is something that hitherto has not been revealed but has been sufficiently revealed to show the unknown even in psycho-analysis: the idea of there being *an* unconscious, as well as a *quality* of unconscious—things are unconscious, we have unconscious feelings and ideas.

It would be as well to consider an unconscious that has never been anything else, has never been conscious. I suspect that a clue to this is given by this theory of Melanie Klein's—projective identification. Even the foetus develops a capacity for what is later called projective identification. In other words, it has feelings or primordial ideas that it tries to deal with by evacuating them—a primitive mechanism derived maybe from the physical capacity for evacuation, literally, so that the amniotic fluid is polluted with meconium. I am suggesting that besides the conscious and unconscious states of mind, there can be another one. The nearest I can get to giving it a provisional title is the *inaccessible* state of mind. It may become inaccessible because the foetus gets rid of it as soon as it can. Whether it is an awareness of its heartbeat, or an awareness of feelings of terror, of sound, or of sight—the kind of sight experienced through the pressure on the optic pits by changes of pressure in the intra-uterine fluid—all that may never have been what we would call either conscious or unconscious. It is difficult to contemplate because when we are contemplating it, we are in a conscious state of mind—like waking up and saying we had a dream. That is an elaboration in a state of mind appropriate to being what we call 'awake'. But the dream took place—if it was a dream—when we were asleep, and that is a quite different state of mind. So the conscious account of this event, these places we went to, these places we saw, is certainly erroneous. It is possibly rational—Freud claims that dreams are rational, that they can be given rational interpretations, which is perfectly true. But that is not of the dream itself. When someone who is wide awake has one of those experiences, we say that he is hallucinated or deluded; that state of mind has not been investigated because it is so much simpler to put that patient into a mental hospital or into an entirely different state of mind by the administration of drugs. And anyway it has to be investigated by somebody who is wide awake, fully conscious, and in possession of all his senses. When I say 'all his senses', I do not mean all of what my contemporaries and what rational and reasonable people call 'senses'; I include senses of which I myself may not be fully or particularly aware—the uncertainty principle, the incompleteness principle. So even the mathematicians cannot help me very much, because I think they themselves have reached a similar impasse in this problem of trying to elaborate what they call rigorous thought or rigorous thinking. I have already touched on this in talking about the fact that a state of rhapsody and expressions of rhapsodic excitement aren't good enough; we do need some sort of discipline, rigour of thought. I haven't said what kind of rigour. I don't think I could. Someday, perhaps now, somebody will be able to. But they have first of all to be acquainted with, and able to recognize, a state of mind that is not adequate. There is not much room for dogmatism or bigotry; that has gone too far; that seems to me to cross the point of no recall. Somebody who is that amount disciplined, or that amount rigorous, or that amount bigoted, is not within reach of the realms about which we need to know more.

Since we are now embarking on a somewhat different theme, we would do well to consider what the theme is that we are embarking upon. It has a great deal to do with this matter of judgement, because by this time we have a lot of information available on which to operate. If we consider for a moment what we gather, what we have the intelligence to be able to gather, how are we to have the wisdom to know which part of this gathered information is worthy of further consideration at the *present time*? What is to put all this material into order—in order of precedence? Who or what chooses or decides or acts as the authority in the person? It may be possible that the matter could be illuminated to some extent by observing . . . [*tape ends*]

REFERENCES

Bion, W. R. (1961). *Experiences in Groups and Other Papers*. London: Tavistock.

Bion, W. R. (1962a). A Theory of Thinking. *International Journal of Psycho-Analysis, 43*: 4–5. [Also in *Second Thoughts: Selected Papers on Psycho-Analysis*. London: Heinemann, 1967; reprinted London: Karnac Books, 1987.]

Bion, W. R. (1962b). *Learning from Experience*. London: Heinemann [reprinted London: Karnac Books, 1984].

Bion, W. R. (1963). *Elements of Psycho-Analysis*. London: Heinemann [reprinted London: Karnac Books, 1984].

Bion, W. R. (1965). *Transformations*. London: Heinemann [reprinted London: Karnac Books, 1984].

Bion, W. R. (1974/75). *Brazilian Lectures*. Rio de Janeiro: Imago Editore [new edition in one volume, London: Karnac Books, 1990].

Bion, W. R. (1977). *Two Papers: The Grid and Caesura*. Rio de Janeiro: Imago Editore [reprinted London: Karnac Books, 1989].

Bion, W. R. (1980). *Bion in New York and São Paulo*. Strathclyde: Clunie Press.

Bion, W. R. (1991). *A Memoir of the Future* (Books 1–3 with 'A Key'). London: Karnac Books.

Bion, W. R. (1994). *Cogitations* (extended edition), ed. F. Bion. London: Karnac Books.

Fitzgerald, E. (1859). Free translation of *The Rubáiyát of Omar Khayyám*.

Ford, Richard (1845). *A Hand-Book for Travellers in Spain, and Readers at Home* (2 volumes). London: John Murray.

Freud, S. (1911b). Formulations on Two Principles of Mental Functioning. *Standard Edition, 12* (pp. 213–226). London: Hogarth Press.

INDEX

Action, as used in Grid, 7, 10
Algebraic Calculus, as used in
      Grid, 7
Alpha:
   -element(s), viii, xi, 29, 30
     as used in Grid, x, 7, 8, 10, 11
   function, 10
Archaic vestigial elements, x, 38,
     44
Aristotle, 9
Attention, as used in Grid, 7, 10
   function of [Freud], 9

Beatriz, R., 3
Beta-element(s), viii, xi, 30, 40
   as 'box', x, 29, 36
   as used in Grid, x, 7, 8, 10, 11
Bion in New York and Sao Paulo, 4
Bizarre objects, 11
'Box', beta-element as, x, 29, 36
Brazilian Lectures, 4
British Psycho-Analytical Society,
     vii, 3
Brouwer, L. E. J., 49

Cantor, G., 49
Categorization of statements, with
     Grid, 8
Charcot, J. B., 35
Circle, ix, xi, 18, 19, 20
Circular argument(s), x, 15, 18–20
   failure of, 18
   fruitful vs. sterile, 19

Classification, 5, 13, 14
   of psychoanalytical objects, vii
Clough, A. H., 43
Cogitations, viii
Communication(s):
   analysis of, 12, 13
   artist's, 13
   over centuries, 33, 42
   difficulty of, 31–34, 48
   mathematical, method of
     recording analogous to, 5,
     6
   modes of, 46
   patient's, 47
   rhythmical, x, 31
Concept, as used in Grid, 7
Conception, as used in Grid, 7,
     17
Constant conjunction, 9, 10, 12,
     16, 18, 19
   and implication of significance,
     9
Counter-transference, viii, 6
Curiosity, 40

Daniel, Book of, dreams in, 28
Definitory hypothesis, as used in
     Grid, 7, 9
Delusion, 41, 50
Denial, 46
Desire and memory, xi
   importance of being rid of,
     43–44

Dream(s), 30, 36
  in Bible, 28
  communication through, 34, 41
  Freud on, 50
  vs. hallucination, 50
  significance of, 28, 29
  -thoughts, as used in Grid, x, 7,
    11
  as used in Grid, 11
  -work-alpha, viii

Edinburgh Conference, 18
Elements of Psycho-Analysis, vii,
    viii, 4
Evaluation, x, 39
Evans, A., 33
Experiences in Groups, ix

Fitzgerald, E., 31, 51
Ford, R., 46, 51
Free associations, 44
Freud, S., 9–11, 17, 28, 35, 37, 49, 50

Game, psycho-analytical, 14, 20
Genesis, Book of, dreams in, 28
Gödel, K., 49
Grating, 4
Grid, vii, 1–21
Guilt, and capacity to lie, 35

H, use of Grid for, 8
Hallucination, 41, 50
Heisenberg, W. K., Uncertainty
    Principle of, 49
Helix, the Grid as, 4
Heyting, A., 49
Hugo, V., 30
Hume, D., 9
Hypothesis, definitory, 7
    definition of term as used in
      Grid, 9

Identification, projective, 49
Imagination, x, 45–49

speculative, x, xi, 40, 41, 46, 47,
    49
  use of in supervision, 45
Incompleteness principle, 49, 50
Inquiry, as used in Grid, vii, 7
Interpretation, 5, 13–14, 17, 19–21,
    28, 40, 50
  and material, 20
  psycho-analytical, vs. meaning,
    14
  as transformation, 14
    and as statement, 13
Intuition:
  development of capacity for, 5,
    21
  training of, 5, 6

Joyce, J., x

K-link, use of Grid for, 8, 14
Kenner, H., 33
Kipling, R., 34
Klein, M., 49

L, use of Grid for, 8
Lancaster, O., 31
Language, kinds of, 46
Learning from Experience, 3, 11
Leonardo da Vinci, 42
Los Angeles Psychoanalytic
    Society, ix

Mathematical communication, 5,
    6, 16, 30, 40
Mathematical counterpart of
    thought, 19
Mathematics, uncertainty in, 49,
    50
Meaning:
  vs. psycho-analytical interpreta-
    tion, 14
  of significant, interpretation of,
    14
Memoir of the Future, A, x

Memory:
 and desire, xi
 importance of being rid of,
  43, 44
 and notation [Freud], 9
Mind:
 archaic vestigial aspects of, x
 state of (conscious, unconscious,
  inaccessible), 50
Model, as used in Grid, 7, 11, 12,
 19
Mozart, W. A., 42
Myth, as used in Grid, 4, 7, 11, 12

Nachträglichkeit, x
No-breast, 19
 and thought, 18
No-penis, 19
Notation, as used in Grid, 7, 10
 and memory [Freud], 9

O, use of Grid for, 12, 13
Object(s):
 bizarre, 11
 psycho-analytical, 15, 16
  classification of, vii
Observation(s), 5, 13–15, 20, 44
 psycho-analytical, 15
 theory of, 15
Oedipus, as used in Grid, vii, viii,
 7, 10
Omar Khayyám, 31

Poincaré, J. H., 9
Pre-conception, as used in Grid, 7,
 11, 15, 17
Projective identification, 49
Psycho-analysis (*passim*):
 minimum conditions for, 43, 45–
 47
Psycho-analytic supervision, x

Reasoning, speculative, xi, 40, 47,
 49

Reconstruction, xi, 49
Resistance, 9

Scientific Deductive System, as
 used in Grid, 7
Shakespeare, W., 30, 32, 33, 42
Speculative imagination, x, xi, 40,
 41, 46, 47, 49
Speculative reasoning, xi, 40, 47,
 49
Speech, articulate, 35
Statement(s), 5, 8–20, 35
 analyst's, Grid used to classify,
 13
 definition of term, 8
 interpretation as, 13
 loose vs. rigorous, 11
 meaningfulness of, 16
 psycho-analysis as, 20
 rightness/wrongness of, 16
 as transformations, 15
 unsaturated, 11
Stravinsky, I. F., 31
Supervision, psychoanalytic, x, 40,
 43, 45

Talamo, P. Bion, vii–xi
Tαa, 12
Tαp, 12, 14
Tβa, 12
Tβp, 12, 13, 14
Theory, 16
 meaning of term as used in
  Grid, 15, 16
 rightness/wrongness of, 15
Thorner, H., 3
Thought(s), *passim*
 archaic, 38
 architectonics of, 40
 development of, patient's, viii
 dream-, x, 11
 and no-breast, 18, 19
 rigorous, 50
 stray, x, 27, 28, 29, 30